NO ROOM AT THE INN

Michael J. Melvin, BEM

MINERVA PRESS
LONDON
MONTREUX LOS ANGELES SYDNEY

NO ROOM AT THE INN

ISBN 1 85863 785 6

First Published 1997 by
MINERVA PRESS
195 Knightsbridge
London SW7 1RE

Printed in Great Britain for Minerva Press

NO ROOM AT THE INN

Cover by the Reverend Jane Taylor

My gratitude to Jane,
whose interpretation of our thoughts
are so well reflected in her
design of the book cover.

Jean Melvin

No use knocking at the window.
Some are hungry, some are not, sir.
We are Christian men and women
But we're keeping what we've got, sir.

Standing in the Rain
Sydney Carter

There is still more light and truth to break forth from His word.

The parting words of
Pastor John Robinson
to the Pilgrim Fathers in 1620

About the Author

Born in Edinburgh in 1924, the young Michael Melvin moved to Glasgow and then West Lothian, where he attended Broxburn High School.

In 1941, following the outbreak of the Second World War, Michael moved to Lancashire with his father, who was in REME (Royal Electrical and Mechanical Engineers). Michael was called up in 1943 to start his naval service, and served on board minesweepers around the British Isles and in the Mediterranean, being promoted to the rank of petty officer, until his demobilisation in 1946. Four years later Michael joined the RAF and over the next nineteen years travelled to all parts of the globe, attaining the rank of flight sergeant after receiving the British Empire medal while a corporal in 1959. During his service in the RAF he became a lay preacher and was credited with sole responsibility for the construction of an interdenominational chapel on the base.

On leaving the RAF in 1969, Michael was ordained into the Congregational Ministry and took up a pastorate in Norfolk, then began a fifteen year ministry in the United Reformed Church in Harlow and Roydon, Essex. Michael's was a very active ministry, and he retained his positions of chaplain to the Royal British Legion, the Royal Naval Association and the Normandy Veterans Association as well as carrying out his duties as Free Church chaplain to the Princess Alexandra Hospital in Harlow, and the position of Wing Chaplain to the Air Training Corps even after his retirement in 1989. Michael actually retained all of these positions after his retirement right up to his death in 1995

The Reverend Michael Melvin became well known in the Harlow area as the minister who would christen every baby for whom Christian baptism was requested and marry any couple who desired a Christian marriage. He had a natural rapport with both young and old, and his rich sense of humour and deep humanity won him many friends.

Michael died from a heart condition on 13th October 1995. He left three sons, nine grandchildren and three great-grandchildren from his first marriage, and his second wife and stepson. He is remembered with great affection by the many people who were fortunate enough to know him.

Contents

Introduction

I am a retired minister of the United Reformed Church, having served that body since its inception in 1972, and before that I was in the Congregational Church, after serving for twenty-two years with Her Majesty's armed services, both in the Royal Navy and the Royal Air Force, where I received, thanks to the liberal-mindedness of many chaplains of differing denominations, on the Free Church side as well as a fair smattering of C of E and Catholic brethren, an introduction to the ecumenical scene.

What I write here has everything to do with people, all sorts of people, of differing denominations, but particularly those who belong to none of the orthodox branches of the church or indeed any of what are sometimes regarded as 'offshoots'. I write of the inward fear of the 'closed shop' attitude I have found to be prevalent in most of the churches of today, including my own, reflecting a growing Calvinistic approach rather than a generous and understanding feeling towards those whom we often regard as standing outside the fold.

From the way some of our churchfolk behave, that is where they are destined to stay.

I have always believed in and treasured the freedom won for us by our forefathers (and mothers, who are sometimes forgotten) which can be and is expressed in the ministry of word and sacrament, but it often comes with a great deal of judgement and criticism.

Equally I have always treasured, as many do, the opportunity of trying as well as I am able to meet the needs of those who from time to time had the courage or cheek to knock on my door and ask for help.

What form that help took differed in many ways, depending very much upon the circumstances, and indeed upon where one, under God's guidance, was led. The aim was always to reflect, as far as one's limitations would allow, something of the abiding love of God, and especially insofar as He has the time not only to care, but to do.

I like to think that any response I ever made to that knocking and seeking was consistent not with the man-made laws of the Church, however good and adequate they are in many circumstances, but with the gospel of love as depicted in the life of Jesus.

This of course has its different interpretations, but it would seem that, in the main, love is not readily available unless the person being loved or needing to be loved can respond in a similar way, and only under the conditions which are laid down: providing you do that you can have this.

I am not unduly bothered about the folk who have already committed themselves to the ways of God. They know or at least profess to know what it is all about, although many would seem to fall short in recognising the implications of God's commands in relation to the community and the world.

What bothers me, and should bother every other God-fearing soul, are those who are still 'outside' (if that is the correct term) the Church, and who, if our attitude does not change, will continue to remain outside.

What I mean is that unless we are prepared to make adequate allowances for those who do not share our convictions, and who in many cases are not even aware of what those convictions are, or indeed whence they stem, we will never make any impression in the community, never mind the world.

What I have to say in the following chapters may be misinterpreted to such a degree that I may very well be regarded as one of the heretics of our day – to be burned at the stake! A rebel of the Nineties. But I tentatively put pen to paper (not for the first time, for this was initially penned in 1978) knowing that many who read it (if any) will understand in some measure what it is I am trying to say in my own stumbling way, and with the profound belief that what I write must be said not in my own defence, nor indeed in the defence of the Church, but in defence of those who are still outside the fold. More often than not it is not their fault, but the fault of those who continually seek to maintain the barriers which do nothing but keep us apart. There is a need to recognise that the Church is not an exclusive but an inclusive organisation.

It is virtually no use quoting chapter and verse at people. Anything beyond John's Gospel and a great deal within the Gospels themselves would seem to me to be quite irrelevant as far as the uninitiated are concerned. The Book of Acts is the story of the early Church, already established with committed or at least interested folk, and certainly God-oriented; while Paul's letters are indeed his own inspired interpretations of the Christian faith as he understood it at the time – his own theology of the life and teaching of Christ, directed not at the heathen, if indeed there are such people, but at those already dedicated souls, the first converts.

There are nine main lines of thought which have become major concerns within the Church in our time, and about which I am at variance with many of my colleagues.

What follows cannot invite calls for my resignation for I am now retired and perhaps freer now to express my views than before, which are offered with a great deal of pain. Having had a few fatherly lectures from those who have deigned to glance at my work, who have reminded me of my sinful ways, it must also be put on record that there are others, very sensible and educated people, but not unfortunately in the Church, who have recommended that I get the book published. They claim that it throws a great deal of light on some of those subjects about which they have 'felt sceptical'.

I trust therefore that some who read this will benefit from the knowledge that someone somewhere thinks and does very much the same as themselves.

Chapter I
Creation and Original Sin

Creation has been the subject of numerous religious writers without counting the secular and the scientific. The concept of original sin is primarily in the sphere of the theologian and the philosopher, and much has been written about that as well. The Bible has little to say, however, about the concept of creation except that behind our existence and indeed, the existence of all which is seen as well as unseen, there is some great power at work whom man in the first instance chose to call God. And he has been doing it ever since.

The Book of Genesis in the Old Testament is simply man's explanation of his own experiences or his own understanding of what has been already revealed and is unfolding before his very eyes. We, in the twentieth century, have to imagine ourselves in the role of someone who lived some two thousand five hundred years ago, grappling with limited knowledge, some of the major philosophical questions which still bamboozle humankind today, and, in all fairness, arriving at what would be regarded then as logical and rational answers, which are as valid today as they were all those years ago, we in the twentieth century having nothing better to offer.

Let us imagine someone whom we might call Joseph, sitting under the roughly made awning of his tent sheltering from the heat of the noonday sun, not in Palestine, but somewhere in the Egyptian desert. Here he is cursing the heat of the day and equally the cold of the night, but also from time to time reflecting on the need for such heat and cold.

'Why can't it all be the same, one thing or the other? It would make life a lot easier?' he asks.

Here he is, with a family and possibly a herd of goats or cattle or maybe just one goat and one cow. Life is simple, quiet, and, apart from the occasional family reunion (he has a brother and sister who seem to live miles away although in modern terms they're only up the road), when it takes about three days' walking and resting to cover the distance, they live very much on their own, travelling a few miles daily in any direction to places they are likely to find enough fodder for their animals. Life is slow, it is undisturbed, and Joseph ponders the great mysteries of life and living and indeed dying.

It's not so mysterious really for he knows where he came from. Straight out of his mother's belly (and a tough time she had too), just like his wife Sarah when the twins were born. That was strange, he had thought, because he was almost certain that he had slept with his other wife that night. But perhaps he had too much of the wine he had acquired at the last market in exchange for some goatskin garments.

Joseph also knows that if he wants to increase his herd of cattle he must introduce Annabel to a bull. So by simple logic he deduces that one must always start with two, a male and a female (and one wonders how long it took the first humans to discover that; possibly by trial and error if the truth is known). If it is true of animals, then it must be equally true for humankind; thus he arrives at the conclusion which would seen simple to us – that two people started the human race.

But how did they get there?

Well, that probably was tied up with the answer to the other questions he has been asking. What questions were those? one might ask. Well, not having a local library or reference books to hand, he is just a trifle bothered about nature and how it came about. The sun comes up and goes down always in the same place and at the same time, the moon shines with a regularity which is most amazing. The rain falls and the plants grow, and there is day and night. And then there is the wind, which seems to come from nowhere, and the occasional oasis where one can find water even on the hottest days. How does one account for all this?

Joseph has in fact consulted all his friends and they seem as confused as he is. They just do not know. Who or what was responsible for all this activity? It is not that Joseph wants to blame anyone, rather that he wants to thank someone, for he knows, does he not, that without food and water both he and his cattle would surely die.

So to whom does Joseph apportion responsibility for these remarkable and most welcome resources, and all free at that?

Something or someone other than Abu ben-Adam down the road, other than all the folks Joseph has already consulted and who categorically deny having anything to do with the gifts of sun and rain and growth. So in some small measure Joseph begins to comprehend a little of the Creator's work, who in his eyes must get the credit for the wonders of the universe.

But there are other things which bother Joseph. There is something wrong with humankind, which is plain enough to see. Has not Asher stolen one of Joseph's goats? And when he was faced with the charge at the market, he denied it. Not only was Asher a thief, he was also a liar, for had he not offered up the animal for sale with Joseph's mark on it? Protestation brought only a bloody nose for poor Joseph.

There is something wrong with mankind to do a thing like that, and more so because late that night Joseph had chosen to give Asher a roughing up.

So it was that, linking all these experiences, plus many others of a similar nature (one guy had even attempted to rape his only daughter), Joseph asks the questions and finds in his own reasoning some realistic and rational answers.

How do we account for our existence; the universe; nature; man's misbehaviour? Joseph concludes that most of this can be attributed to none other than a power greater than himself – which to my mind is the result of simple, rational and logical thought: beginning, as it were, to grasp the reality of something that has already been revealed in the universe where he is, and which he came eventually to know as God.

God created the universe. Yes, that is possible. The land, the sea and the air. Indeed, yes. And the animals and the birds, and day and night, the sun, the moon, the stars, the rain and everything that man can see? Yes, that is a feasible conclusion. A good God to provide all these things: a place in which to live; land to till; seed to grow; animals, fish and birds to help sustain us; and man to have dominion over all these things. Man, the supreme earthly being, able to think and do; and indeed create in his own small way. Nothing of course as great and as mighty as his God, but, nevertheless, with an ability which makes him different from the rest of the animal kingdom. A good God indeed, a creator who commands reverence, loyalty and worship: someone to whom a simple man like Joseph and his family could give thanks.

But what about this other thing? Man's destructive capacity: this hatred, prejudice, jealousy; this corruption of the body made in the likeness of a good God. Where does this fit into the scene? Somehow Joseph has to account for this bad streak in human nature.

It does not appear possible that a good God who commands worship and adoration can be responsible for this ugly twist in man's nature. Indeed not!

But who to blame? Mankind? By no means. After all, we wish nobody any harm, unless of course they harm us first. Only then do we retaliate and this is strictly a question of self-preservation, is it not? We cannot allow every Tom, Dick, Harry, Mary or Jean to go around creating difficult and awkward situations, upsetting folk and causing unnecessary problems. No, we must find another scapegoat for the sins of the world.

Nor would it be fair to put the blame on the helpmate Joseph has been given; that would not be right. Rather blame someone or something which cannot defend itself – the serpent, the Biblical symbol of deceit, the arch-deceiver. And what could be much lower than a snake? He could take the blame, and so it was that in the opening chapters of Scripture we find the earliest concept of what we, in our own time, might call 'passing the buck'; that is, man, because of his unwillingness to accept the responsibility for his own actions, shifts the burden of blame on to the shoulders (or in, this case the back) of a poor defenceless animal.

There, as far as the writer is concerned, the matter ends, concluding what might be regarded as both a rational and logical explanation of man's own condition as he understood it at the time. No better could be found, and it helped to explain many factors which had previously been couched in mystery. This explanation seemed to adequately satisfy the intellect of the day, when man had begun to perceive some of the truths God was revealing about the human condition.

The doctrine of original sin is said to have derived from the third chapter of the Book of Genesis, but there is no foundation for such a doctrine in Scripture. The fact of sin yes, and we would all recognise that today, if not in ourselves then most certainly in someone else (here we go again, just like our ancestors, passing the buck). Not me sir, but him.

The truth of course is that God, in creating mankind with a free will, made evil possible. That makes mankind responsible. Good or evil is *our* choice, unlike the assertion of our old friend Rabbie Burns, who claims in one of his poems that the responsibility for his own actions lies not with him but the God who made him. We could all say that of course, but then we would be nothing but a bunch of robots, dangling like puppets on the end of a string.

This of course fits in neatly with St Augustine's theory of predestination, based upon Paul's statement in his letter to the Church in Rome that those who have not been chosen might as well give up trying, a doctrine which cannot, however, be reconciled with the kind of love Jesus portrayed during his ministry and more so on the cross.

"Father, forgive them for they know not what they do."

A love that was unconditional, expressing the view that whatever we do it will not change God's love for us, for the simple reason that, made as we are in the image of God, we are his family, created just a little lower than the angels, and for whom the very hairs on our head are numbered.

"Would you give your son a stone if he asks for bread?" asked Jesus. No indeed, and neither will your father in heaven.

Whatever else the Bible says, it screams about the uniqueness of mankind, the value of the human being, and about the place he holds in the scheme of things.

Man is God's prime concern and page after page of the Bible remind us of this fact, about the lengths to which He has gone and is prepared to go for us.

It is a poor analogy, but we might compare ourselves with a thermometer, rising and falling a few degrees as we respond and indeed reject the will and love of God while we seek to maintain, wittingly or otherwise, the standards set by Christ. We all do it one way or another even if we do not recognise that we are doing God's work. The mercury never reaches the bottom, nor does it ever reach maximum on the scale; indeed it does not ever disappear from the gauge. So we come into this world at blood temperature and as we go through life we gain or lose a few degrees, some gaining or losing more than others, but never leaving this world without any.

In the light of Jesus's teaching and his claim that he came to show us what God is like, it is difficult to believe that God can have no mercy at all, even for the most wicked, and this is surely borne out in our own experience.

As human beings we can forgive people the most despicable things. Fathers have declared forgiveness for those who have murdered their nearest and dearest, as indeed mothers have done. Surely God, who is much greater than us all, and indeed much more loving, can do that much more than we can ever imagine possible?

This is not to say that there can be no judgement. What kind of mansion we get when we finally reach the other side of the river is not for us to decide, but one there will surely be. If this is not the case, then God has hoodwinked at least one of those he claims to love.

God loves us not for what we are likely to become but for what we are now. The story of the prodigal son reminds us that, whether he returned home or not, God still cared for him.

Chapter II
Election

'You Have Not Chosen Me, I Have Chosen You'

The concept of election has always troubled me, and no doubt many others as well, because it is essentially linked with the question of individual choice. The theological answer, some would say, to the question, 'Why am I a minister of the gospel?' or indeed, 'Why am I a Christian?', is simply 'I have been chosen'. What must inevitably follow those questions is another just as important: 'Why me and not him or her? What special qualities, if any, have I which mark me out as one of God's favourites, that I should be chosen any more than Joe Bloggs or Annie Jones?'

There are of course many references in Scripture which relate to this whole concept of 'the chosen'. We are told and indeed reminded time and time again that the Israelites were the chosen people of God, that the prophets were chosen for specific reasons, meaning to be God's agents (though somewhat reluctantly) of his mercy and justice in his world.

I believe that this word 'chosen' builds a picture of self-righteousness which tends to separate us from the rest of society, and which certainly separated the Jews from other cultures. It presents the kind of picture suggesting that those of us who are committed to the ways of Christ ('how far?' is a serious question too) have somehow found favour with the Almighty (and I cannot for the life of me think why), because it is so destined. God finds special qualities in our make-up which mark us out as particular members of his flock, and a limited flock at that according to some, and a flock, because of these limitations, to which I do not have any desire to belong.

Commentators say a great deal about this idea of the chosen race, Jesus reminds us that 'many are called, but few are chosen', a phrase which would appear to spell out that there are some clearly marked out for specialist treatment, but if we imply that 'chosen' means we are in some way specially selected, then it must also mean, in addition to the fact that others are specially rejected, that we have no individual choice in the matter, we have no freedom – we are marked men and women before we are conceived, and for reasons known only to the Lord himself we have been favoured or rejected.

It must also mean that without choice we are puppets, and that those who are not included in the fold are free, as we who have been chosen are not free. And if we are not free but controlled, why is it that we fail miserably to do all those things we are commanded to do, or be all that we are supposed to be?

I believe that in large measure we are up the creek without a paddle, much the same as Paul was in his time. I believe that the problem lies in our misinterpretation of the meaning of the word 'chosen', as indeed the Biblical writers did before us, taking it to mean selected in an individual and nationalistic manner rather than in a corporate way.

The Book of Genesis reminds us that mankind, not simply Tom Smith or Mary MacDonald or Sarah Thompson, was created in the image of God, and if we believe in God as creator then we must, of necessity, be concerned with all creatures.

The question is, 'What value is there in the flesh and bone of human society in a worldly sense? Who is Mary Smith and who is Joe Bloggs? Have they a place in the scheme of things or are they merely numbers on a computer to be used and manipulated, then discarded when the need arises, to be slung on the dust heap of redundancy?'

Jesus put his stamp on the value of mankind: the outcast; the vagabond; the thief; the traitor; those of different faiths and none; the children; the sick, the maimed and the blind. In all, the average man and woman in the street. Whatever or whoever you are, Jesus is saying, God has time for you, God cares about you, so lift up your head, stand up on your feet and be counted. He saw, while we often fail to see, in each and every soul – yes, even in the Sadducees and Pharisees, even in Judas who betrayed him and in Peter who denied him – an image of the God who created us all.

In this sense I believe that we have been chosen, destined if you like, to be what we are; not cats or dogs, not puppets or robots, but responsive human beings.

The word responsive is important for it implies freedom of choice, it implies being close to or away from God. In that same Book of Deuteronomy 30:5 God is made to say 'therefore I set before you this day good and evil, therefore choose good that you may live long in the land.' And going back to our origins in mythical Adam, he too was given a choice.

We are not to know why it is that the tree of knowledge was forbidden, but I have a shrewd suspicion that the writer knew, as well as we all know, that knowledge can and often does lead to the setting up of our own gods, or indeed leads us to set ourselves up as gods or perhaps be regarded by others as gods, in opposition to our creator. So it is that Adam knew the score when he was tempted. The choice was his, as indeed were the consequences of that choice.

To be chosen by God does not mean that there is no human choice; a management committee can choose eleven players for a football team, but they do not have to play. Of course they can be made to play by threatening them with losing their place or indeed their job, but if that is management's way then it is certainly not the way of God, although it has appeared to be so in many instances with threats of hell and the 'burning fire'.

Mankind is a chosen race in that, so far as we are aware, there is no other race like us in the whole expanse of the universe. This makes us unique: this makes everybody special, different, chosen for a purpose, for intimate fellowship with God. To say that Abraham was specially chosen is one thing, but it remained for him to respond. We can never be sure how many were called to be prophets. What we do know is that some responded, that others were removed because they did not conform and that not a few of them were reluctant recruits, with Paul in the New Testament being, as it were, in the front rank.

All could have said no, as indeed some of them did to begin with. Indeed we must allow that they had the opportunity to refuse the 'call' otherwise we deny them the freedom which Jesus himself bought at such a price.

And talking of Jesus, we do claim that he went to the cross of his own choosing, therefore we need to accord the same measure of freedom to those he came to serve. Israel was a reluctant respondent, and the choice, if one looks at it closely enough, and if the Jews were chosen in the way they have always claimed, was on God's part a bad one. He had a devil of a time with them. They took many years to 'catch on', with countless rebellions on the way. In many ways they never did 'catch on' in spite of the exhortations and the many chances afforded them along the way.

The truth, however, would seem to be that these were the people who were most able to respond, to give some account of their background of faith for their existence, reasons for their behaviour and the introduction of a moral code; the people who were perhaps the first to find logical and rational answers to the puzzling questions to face them in their time, like, 'What am I doing here? Who am I? How did this world come into existence?' and point in the direction of one God who created it all. Other people in different parts of the world at that time were probably asking the same questions and producing different answers. It is only now, as a result of archaeological discovery and intensive enquiry into the origins of other cultures that we are beginning to understand something of the thinking of those outside the regions of Jewish and Christian thought.

The call of each leader of the Jews must have involved choice, and it may very well have been that, since no one else wanted the job, but they felt God's work was important and someone had to do it, these leaders were willing to do it. We have all felt like that at times. 'The harvest is plentiful but the labourers are few.' (Matthew 9:37.)

Likewise it must have been for those of the New Testament era, who committed themselves to the way of the cross (and cross it would have been for most). To follow Jesus meant responding at some level, for, after all, the disciples were neither robots nor puppets but able and professional men. Indeed the whole of Jesus's ministry was one of choice at every stage. He was Himself called. He was chosen yes, but the story of the temptations, of his agony in the Garden of Gethsemane, are proof enough that he need not have gone God's way: 'Let this cup be taken away from me.' (Matthew 26:39.)

We claim that Jesus faced the crucifixion willingly, that for Jesus the road to Calvary meant real sacrifice, the giving of Himself voluntarily, yet for some reason or another we claim equally that we have been specially chosen with no choice of our own, saying that in some mysterious way we are the 'elect'.

This surely was the failure of the Jews, for did they not take God and entrench him in a narrow, bigoted self-righteous exclusiveness? It took Jesus, a deliberate act of God through Him, to burst asunder the notion that the Jews were anything special. They were no more special than anyone else.

"I have come that you may have life. You are the light of the world. The very hairs of your head are numbered," said Jesus. This was a call to every man, woman and child, and he set out to break the chains that bound society in narrow systems and regulations. It was an endeavour doomed to failure, attempting to sweep away the tangle of cobwebs slowly choking the love and mercy of God, and this in spite of the many voices crying in the wilderness, like those of Isaiah, Ruth and Jonah. They were barking, so to speak, up the wrong tree. Jesus wept for them, but they were too entangled in their nationalism and its rules to take much heed.

So the emphasis turned on the gentile world, where Jesus's message was receiving a fair measure of response. But the lesson was not learned. The Church is still regarded as that chosen by God, when the truth is that it is no more than an instrument of God's love and care in the world. It is no more special than the Jews were or are. Those within its walls are those who are privileged to have experienced and recognised the love of God in their lives, and the truth must surely be that when the question, 'Why me and not him?' is asked it is simply that he has not seen the whole of God in the same light, that we have perhaps started from different places and backgrounds, and that we are privileged through our upbringing and the knowledge which has been imparted to us or which we have attained on life's journey.

There are others who have had much the same advantages, but who have failed to respond, possibly because they have seen no need for religion, or because those of us who have been so privileged have failed to get the message across in such a way to encourage rather than chase people away. But they too have been chosen or called, because, in a word, they are members of the one family, the human race, created in God's image.

When the Psalmist asks the question 'What is man?' and he replies that 'He has been created just a little lower than Yourself and appointed him over everything You have made,' who in fact is he talking about? The Christian? The Jew? Neither, but the whole of humankind. When Jesus talks about the children coming to him, to what children is he referring? The children of practising believers? I would guess not. When he talks about the hairs in our head being numbered, is he concerned only with the committed? Does not God care for the whole mass of heaving, sighing and mixed-up society? If he does not, then does not this make his love conditional? If we are destined to be chosen before we were born, what purpose was there in Jesus coming at all? What is the point of evangelism if God has already chosen those he wills to be his own? They will have been chosen anyway or rejected, in spite of any puny effort we choose to make, and which will be for no purpose anyway. Is the lack of response to the many evangelistic efforts made in the name of Christ an indication that God has rejected those whom we would seek to bring into the fellowship of the Church?

Such questions bother me and cause me to reject this whole concept of election. If I have been elected, then it is only in the sense that I belong, as indeed all human beings belong, to a very special part of God's creation, and this makes me, together with all my fellow men and women, important to God. If I am called to follow Christ then because I have free will I can just as well reject that call as accept it. Indeed some of my colleagues, having responded to a call to enter the ministry of the Church, have now opted out, for reasons only known to themselves. That is not God's choice, it is theirs.

That, however, will not stop God loving them any more than it stops a loving father or mother caring for a son or daughter who has forgotten their existence. God's love is not dependent upon how we act, but the way we behave enhances or hinders the community in which we live. It can therefore have an adverse effect on the building of the kind of world community God desires, where each and every soul has his or her rightful place.

Chapter III
Infant Baptism

No one would argue that baptism, as recorded in the New Testament, was practised in large measure by John the Baptist and the disciples. Jesus was baptised by John but there is no record of Jesus performing this ceremony, nor is there any record of the disciples being baptised. The Gospels appear to put greater emphasis on the baptism of the spirit. In the early Church baptism by immersion seems to have been an outward sign of repentance, a symbol of getting rid of the old life and putting on the new, a washing away of one's sins of the past and making a fresh start in a life under the guidance of God, with Jesus as the intermediary. Whether this is what Jesus meant by baptism is open to question. The rite must have been introduced prior to Jesus's arrival on the scene, but there is no record of such a practice in the Old Testament. It is thought in some quarters to have developed as a parallel to the Jewish practice of circumcision. The rite is still performed today in the Baptist and Churches of Christ traditions although it is known that others do likewise, and basically is a public confession of faith.

The Gospels do not relate baptism with any kind of Church; indeed there was certainly no Christian Church to which anyone could belong. The only documentary reference about any practice like the form of baptism used today in Christian Churches is in the twenty-eighth chapter of Matthew where Jesus asks his disciples to baptise in the name of the Father and Holy Spirit, which is a phrase developed later in relation to the doctrine of the Trinity and thought to have been added at a later date.

What concerns me, however, is this sacrament we call infant baptism. Where did it all start? The truth is that we do not know. There is no Scriptural evidence to say that it was done at the time of Jesus's ministry. The one exception which implies that babies might have been included in the baptism of whole families is contained in The Acts of the Apostles, Chapter 16, when the jailer asks, 'Sirs, what must I do to be saved?'

And the answer comes, 'Believe in the Lord Jesus Christ and you will be saved – you and your family.'

He and all his family were baptised at once, and there is no reference to any of the family making their own confession of faith. He must have spoken on their behalf. The family may or may not have included children.

Some, as I have said, have made the parallel with circumcision and so it might be, but if this is the right interpretation then the question must be asked, 'Was Jesus re-baptised in the River Jordan, after being circumcised as a Jewish boy?'

The problem with us today, however, is that those who have no religious background at all still come seeking something spiritual (and they may not know what it is) for their child. What are we to do with them? Better to ask the question, 'What are we to do *for* them?' at this particular stage in their domestic and spiritual life.

To suggest that these folk should go through some kind of course of instruction before their request can be entertained is a lunacy of the highest order, and tantamount to what can only be described as spiritual blackmail. What can five, six or even twelve weeks of regular attendance at church do for such folk? They would be lucky if the subject was touched on but once. Can anyone ever grasp, never mind understand, what faith in Jesus means even after twelve lectures on the subject, which can at best merely touch the surface?

Many of us who have been in the business for a number of years still find the sacrament of infant baptism a difficult subject, particularly because there is a great deal of disagreement about its meaning. Can we really expect the rank outsider, whose knowledge even of the hymns we sing is limited to about three including *Jerusalem*, to openly confess Christ as Lord and Saviour and, as our orders of service, promise to bring their children up in the 'faith and admonition of the Lord'? This is one of the most serious promises anyone is ever likely to make, and we should not therefore expect, nay, we *dare* not ask any family who has not given the matter serious thought to affirm such promises. It becomes a nonsense when many do make such a confession, but with their tongue in their cheek. So what do we do in such circumstances?

Do we say that unless at least one of the parents can satisfy the conditions, as advocated in many of our publications, we are sorry but we can do nothing? Is this really the Christian way for the Church to behave, when Jesus rebuked his disciples for failing to allow the children to come to him? Is this the way to follow the Master who exhorts his people to ask, seek and knock? What is the point if there is nothing to find?

Would any of you who are fathers give your son a stone when he asks for bread? God wouldn't, so neither should we. What is their motive? we ask. Is the motive really important? They are asking with faith which is often as small as a mustard seed, which is many more times non-existent for their child - who is also a child of God - not after he or she has been baptised or made their own confession of faith, before the child can comprehend the implications of this decision. Is the grace of God to be denied? Do we stand in judgement and state by our actions that God is only concerned about those who can recite the appropriate formula or pass the necessary tests? Are we the custodians of God's grace? When we say that the love of God is unconditional do we mean yes, but always subject to the rules and regulations of men and women? These on the whole are well intended, but do a great deal to create unnecessary barriers for those for whom Jesus cares. Doing it on our terms or not at all has been a policy of disaster.

We talk of creative relationships, but can we conscientiously help create any kind of lasting relationship when we throw people in at the deep end of the pool, a fault illustrated perfectly by Leo Rosten in his book *The Joys of Yiddish*? He writes about the ageing Jew who was knocked down by a car outside a city church. A priest came out and offered the last rites. 'Do you believe in God the Father, God the Son and God the Holy Ghost?' The old man replies, 'Here am I dying and he talks to me in riddles.'

In like manner our services, perfectly all right for those who understand the language and are committed to the cause, are riddles to the common folk. One instance will suffice. The writer attended a normal service where there were three baptisms taking place. The families were present and the church was full to overflowing. There were five hymns and the writer, who knows a hymn or two, knew just one. What does this say for the newcomers who simply stood there with mouths firmly shut? The service was not modified in any way to accommodate these families and it is certain that any hope of their returning was completely dashed.

What these good folks are seeking they are not quite sure about, but they do come with a certain measure of faith, which, in a day when the Church is ridiculed and criticised on all fronts, is to be welcomed. If the day ever comes when people stop asking – and it is happening in many quarters where people have had a raw deal or not a very nice experience – then we may as well shut up because by that we will be wholly identified with the closed shop attitude. People will be saying in their thousands what they are at the moment saying in their hundreds: the Church does not want to know,

I have often tried to imagine myself as a total stranger to the church, and as the late William Barclay put it, 'tried to get right inside the skin of the person in order to understand him or her better.' I have sought to see the Church from the outsider's point of view: entering a building with which one is totally unfamiliar, being greeted, if at all, by a lukewarm handshake then sitting on a hard seat and scrutinising a book which one has never seen before. Then someone arrives who is dressed more like the devil than anything else, and announces that we are going to sing a hymn. The words are bad enough, but the *tune*! Never heard anything like it.

I attended one particular church of my own denomination on three consecutive Sundays, had a cup of tea in the hall, where I had to serve myself, and then went home without as much as a hello from anyone.

Hypothetical and not likely to happen in our time we say, but have you ever come across anyone who did not know what a hymn is? I have.

For the majority of those seeking baptism for their children, our orders of service are, to say the least, alien. Of course we can deny them the rite, or indeed offer it with strings which feel like ropes around their neck. Or we can offer the alternative which, in effect, is just the same only couched in different phraseology. That, however, is not the way to start a creative relationship, at least not to my mind. Again one instance among many will suffice.

A young lady appears one night with a baby in her arms. It is raining and she has walked three miles from the town. She says that she has come to see about her baby being 'christened'. I had never seen her before. A cup of tea and a warm fire helps the situation. We talk and make arrangements for the baptism, but then she breaks down, says that her husband has left her and asks if the service will still take place. I assure her that nothing has changed, and on the Saturday before the service she rings to say that her husband has come back and that he would like to come to the church. No, they are not now regular members of the church, but we are good friends and the family is together. I like to think that this came about because she was free to come without any ecclesiastical paraphernalia and 'conditions'; and since that occasion, her niece has become a church member. Who knows what damage might have been done had insuperable barriers been put in that young woman's way at that particular critical time of her life?

The need, in my humble opinion, is to alter the order of service to suit the situation. There is just no argument for denying infant baptism, for giving the children of professing parents preferential treatment, for indeed the grace of God never is or never can be dependent upon a profession of faith, either by the parents or indeed by the minister or priest or congregation for that matter.

And is not the presentation of a child to God in baptism a profession of faith in itself? Surely it must take some measure of faith even to ask; that grain of mustard seed about which Jesus speaks? Who are we, one might ask, to deny anything of a spiritual nature to a child? If infant baptism is rooted in our Church traditions, and I, for one, am for it, then it must be made available to all children and not to a selected few whose parents can honestly make the declaration of faith which the Church requires.

If it is the desire or wish of the parents that Mary or John should come to learn about and know Jesus, by whatever means, then surely this is sufficient for the moment. If they are asked to do their best, and it would appear that all parents want to do just that, without making any rash promises – which they feel (and indeed we feel) they may not be able to fulfil – and within the knowledge and understanding that they already possess, if any, then surely they cannot be expected to do much more. And if promises are what is needed, then it would be incumbent upon the Church, which professes to know most of the answers, to do so on behalf of the family. It is the Church upon whose shoulders lies the responsibility to make and keep contact with the family, and if at the end of the day (and that could be months or even years) there is no response, if that is what is needed, so what? Because they have not come into the active fellowship of the Church are they are lost to God? Now that would be putting limits on God's grace, would it not?

To have the encounter with the family would be an exercise in real ministry, the caring for people, who, for reasons unknown, do not join us on Sunday mornings. We cannot win people by legislation, rules and regulations. We cannot impose standards upon folk. They have to accept them for themselves, and they have to learn, like most of us had to learn, slowly, what those standards are. To refuse infant baptism because parents cannot conform, or indeed because they cannot find godparents who have been confirmed (and they have no desire that the Church should supply this requirement) is tantamount to spiritual blackmail. It can do nothing but create barriers. People need to be encouraged and it is the Church's task to do it. If in the end the seed falls on stony ground, then we have done no harm, but rather given the church an exercise in pastoralia, which, in addition to making the family happier and doing a positive good, has probably found us some good friends.

'Thank you for the lovely service,' someone wrote. 'We all understood every word, and my friends (all twenty-five of them), who have never been in Church before, thought it was wonderful.' That to my mind is ministry. If they choose not to return, should we not be concerned? Certainly, but that is not the crux of the matter; 'as you have done unto the least of my children, so you have done for me', is the criteria upon which we are judged. We must not and cannot stand in judgement. Having met their need, and not minimised the importance of infant baptism in the life of the child and indeed the influence on the parents and those who attend, we can do no more but keep in touch. The seed has been sown, and some of it does take root and grow.

The truth of the matter is that in asking for this sacrament for their child, the parents are inviting God to participate in their family affairs, and to refuse is, in effect, to keep God out. In allowing the child to be brought without any strings attached, meaning without imposing a bewildering array of conditions, we are showing that God does care, that He loves us whether we respond or not; this is the God Jesus reveals to me and I am sure to many others, and the God whom people will want to get to know better. God indeed has their request in love, He has entered a home by invitation, He has been met by people who recognise that this must be so, and who are prepared to confess that they have had at least one experience of the living God, who has for some time appeared to be dead, but who has accepted them and their child just as they are. We must never be left in the position where people have to say that God has never done anything for them. In baptising their children the ball is then passed into their court. What they do with it is entirely up to them, but they cannot ever say that God has failed to respond to their particular need.

I close this chapter with a question. If baptism is to be regarded as that important, why is it that it was not seen to be particularly relevant in the case of those closest to Jesus: the disciples? There is no record of their ever having been baptised.

Chapter IV
Remarriage

First it must be stated in my own defence that I do firmly believe in the sanctity of marriage, that it is or indeed ought to be a lifelong bond between two people, and that for those who enter into it the marriage vows be taken to mean just what they say, meaning that they should not be taken lightly.

Having said that, however, there is a need to recognise that in this year of grace we are faced with a growing number of people for whom marriage has become not a joy but a tragedy. There is no need to go into the reasons why, but we have to accept that there are in this world, and right on our own doorsteps at that, people for whom marriage has been a disaster, ending unfortunately and in spite of a great deal of effort to heal the breach, in the divorce courts.

Of course, I believe that it is the duty of the Church to try and help such breakdowns. If there is a real desire for reconciliation, then we ought to be able to help. In the main we are seldom consulted until it is too late. If we are, it is often at a stage when no conciliatory steps are possible. The unhappy episode for husband, wife and children (and, make no mistake, divorce proceedings seldom produce happy occasions) is then brought to a close.

In addition I also believe that it is the duty of the Church to advocate divorce, certainly in circumstances where it seems as if the two contestants (for that is indeed what they have become, however well they started) cannot be reconciled. I have on one occasion offered this kind of advice as being the right thing in the sight of God for the people in question. On other occasions I have condoned divorce because there was nothing anyone, not even God, could do to make it work, and knowing in my own mind that there was no way any kind of reunion could take place. We cannot hope to keep people together under duress, even for the sake of the children. That has become a recognised fact in the world even if the Churches are loath to accept it. Perhaps in some circumstances remaining together might be the solution but that is not always practicable, and depends very much upon the attitude of the parties involved.

The truth is that we have a large percentage of people in our country who are alone, men and women known as divorcé(e)s, for whom the church has apparently little or no time. They are the souls who because of mistakes, deliberate or otherwise, made in the past have to remain in a state of limbo as far as the Church is concerned, without forgiveness, who stand condemned, having committed in the eyes of the Church the sin of all sins. Let me tell you about John, who is only one of the many whom I have had the privilege of knowing over the years.

He and his girlfriend arrived at the manse (the minister's abode) one cold winter's evening. They wanted to be married in church. They belonged to the Church of England and, because John's first marriage had ended in disaster, he had been denied the ceremony in every Church of England church in the town (about twelve). Clergy were sympathetic, but Church law says no remarriage. 'I feel like an outcast,' said John.

Now he is happily married, and no, they do not come to church, but they do know that God had some time for them, time to meet their particular need. Churches can be and often are inconsistent where remarriage is concerned, for in my own experience I know of couples remarried either in a registry office or in a free church where rules are not so much the order of the day, although some of them can be very sticky at times, and who are now communicant members, mark you, in one of the same churches which refused to marry them.

In any case how is one to know that people have been remarried? Are we to submit all those who seek to enter the church to some kind of questionnaire about their past? For all we know there are probably dozens of couples already within the walls of the Church who have been remarried. In truth, if one were to stand by the law of the Church of England, then they should not be there. If priests are turning a blind eye, and many do remarry divorcés in spite of the law, then should not the law be changed? And indeed there are others who, on occasions, visit places like St Paul's in London and wish, no indeed, pray that the instruments of God's mercy might have some regard for their spiritual needs.

Many of my own colleagues will consider marrying divorcés, but only when they have investigated the whys and wherefores of the breakdown, only when they have subjected those who have come for some help and understanding to a form of third degree examination to ascertain the facts. And what is the point of that, one wonders? To find the truth? We will consent to marry the non-guilty person, they say. How do we start finding out who is what without digging up the past, which most people in such circumstances want to forget? This kind of investigation can be nothing but a mockery, and can only bring about a sense of guilt which has no place in a remarriage.

In any case, who are we to stand in judgement? Even if we knew all the facts (which we cannot know without consulting the previous partner), it is doubtful in the extreme whether the truth would be revealed. If private investigations and solicitors and judges cannot get to the truth, how do we expect to find it? Only God knows the truth and we are not God, neither are we private investigators. Who are we, anyway, to stand in the way of God's forgiveness? Who are we to deny what can only be an expression of God's love to those who come seeking and knocking? They don't all come, but for those who do, surely this demands some measure of faith just to ask, especially in a day and age when people are not asking as they used to.

Janet and Robert come asking for a church wedding. We go through the preliminaries, having agreed that the wedding should take place on a certain day. When I ask them their respective names and addresses (note that the time and date has already been fixed), Janet bursts into tears and gets up to leave the room.

"I suppose that's the end of it then!" she sobs. "We didn't tell you that we are living at the same address."

My response to that was simply that, in a situation where two people are living together and decide that they want to make it permanent, then of all things seeking the assistance of the Church to make it what they can only describe as 'right' is for me is a miracle which causes me to jump for joy. After all, there are many couples who get married in church about whom we know very little and who could very well be living together without our knowledge. The parents' address can be used to indicate otherwise.

Remarriage in church can be, and very often is, a means of grace in a day when God seems to most people to be totally inactive in a predominantly secular Britain.

Such people have made a mistake. So what? Who has not done that in their lifetime? Most of us get away with it, while many are never found out, but with the business of marriage we must ask the question, 'Do people have to live with their mistakes for ever?' Oftimes it has nothing to do with making mistakes, but boils down to sins of omission, as in the writer's case. There is no deliberate act of selfishness on either side, but probably what can be described as neglect of what has been the most important factor in one's life, caused often by the demands of society on one's time. The lesson is often learned when it is too late, and parting is the only sensible solution.

The tragedy for the divorcé(e) is that he (or she) has to go cap in hand for help and in the process reveal all to public view: family trauma, social services, solicitors and court cases which never appear to end. Then they come seeking a fresh start, often with a bunch of kids looking for a new mum or dad, and a renewal of family life with some sort of stability.

'Why do you come?' one asks.

'We're not quite sure, but we think God ought to be in it somewhere.'

And surely this must be a sign to go ahead. After all, these folks are not from Las Vegas with a dozen or so husbands or wives to their credit. No, in the main they are simple folks looking for a bit of security and happiness, having survived the chaos of family breakdown, but because the woman has shelved her husband (which is not permitted; better to continue being a battered wife) and has the mistaken notion, as some would put it, that she can find some measure of happiness with some other fellow (which of course is adultery), the Church does not want to know.

But the miracle is that she does find happiness, and they do live together. They do go for divorce and they do get married, even if it is only in the registry office, which most of them do not want, but for them it is often the only choice. When such people ask the Church for help, this must be welcomed, especially when very few people are asking the Church for anything these days. Is this not a time for creative relationships? If we will not or cannot make a positive response to their request then there is little likelihood of their ever coming back.

That, we hear someone say, is their choice. No, it is our choice, because we are supposed to be the loving, concerned and helpful community. They see the Church not as a support in time of trouble, but as a hindrance to their future happiness, which at that time is all that appears to matter to them.

My own case is a typical example. I had been separated from my wife for three years, with an earnest desire to make things up. It was not to be. I met someone else, proceeded over a long period of time with a do-it-yourself divorce (I could not afford the legal fees), then sought to arrange our marriage. Discussing the question of remarriage at our college's church in Cambridge, only one of my ten colleagues was prepared to do the wedding, and the reason was that I happened to wear a dog collar. They stood in judgement, and had it not been for my moderator, who had more forgiveness and understanding in the tip of his finger than they had together, I would not be in the Church now. He saved the day and my wife and I shall always remember him for showing us that God really did care for our condition, but, more than that, wanted to do something positive about it. I regard myself no more special than all these other folk who ask for the same kind of sympathy and love.

There is a great deal in the Church which smacks of spiritual blackmail: 'we will do this for you providing that...' and then go on to enumerate a list of conditions which must be fulfilled before anything is done.

The love of God in Christ is without conditions, and we have no right to deny God taking an active part in the lives of those who often seek at length to find him. As often happens, the door is not simply slammed, it is not even opened. Just as visiting the sick or counselling the offender, just as helping the poor and comforting the sad is God at work in his world, so too is marrying the divorced. In practically every situation in which I have been involved, people have come to realise that they have experienced God at work not in some remote corner of the earth, but in their very own situation. What they choose to do about it must remain for them to decide, but in many cases these folk are the only contact we have with the community and what makes it tick. And the sad thing is that the Church is very often out of step and equally out of time.

All the words of Scripture, all the hymns we sing, all the prayers we offer and all the sermons we preach come to nothing if we deny the needs of people such as these who, perhaps through no fault of their own, find themselves in a category where they are destined to stay for the remainder of their lives by the authority of man, and without the blessing of God.

We are being taken for a ride, we are told, if we marry folks who have no intention of coming to church. We are being used. So what? Was Jesus never used in his ministry? Where, one might ask, were all those dedicated baptised souls when the crunch came at Calvary?

They will never come back or look at the road you are on. Where were the other nine lepers who were healed by Jesus, when only one came back to say thanks? How many people came to Jesus simply to get what they wanted? Did he turn any of them away? If so I do not recall having read about it. And where were the disciples at the end of the day? They scampered off up the road and left their master to meet his death alone.

One question that always intrigues me is this. What happens to the man or woman who, having been divorced, becomes a Christian and wishes to marry another Christian? Is there no forgiveness for them? I am sure that God, so unlike his Church in many ways, would have little hesitation in welcoming them home.

Chapter V
The Lord's Supper

The Sacrament of Holy Communion, or the Eucharist or Lord's Supper, as some prefer to call it, has, it would seem, always been something of an exclusive affair. The first communion generally follows an act of confirmation or reception into the Church as a member; that is a personal profession of faith. Confirmation and Church membership should, so we are told, be the result of growth and development in the Christian faith, beginning with infant baptism or, in the case of the Baptist Church, total immersion.

It has always been held that, if the parents of a child fulfil their promises made at the child's baptism, namely to 'bring up the child in the faith and admonition of the Lord', the subsequent result of that promise should be Christian training either in Sunday School or Church, culminating in a public profession of faith at a special service. This has generally been the norm in most denominations. This is followed by the new member's first communion, when the invitation is given to 'all those who love the Lord Jesus Christ'.

There has, however, been an increasing awareness in some Churches of the need to include children in this central act of Christian worship, and it has been questioned whether or not they have the right to do so, on the grounds that the children do not know what it is all about. There also arises the question of interpretation. What many people are not aware of is the fact that views differ on where the practice began, even in the New Testament. Saint John's Gospel, for instance, places the time of Jesus's crucifixion the day *before* the Passover and it appears that the concept of sacrifice relating to the communion service in the New Testament arose because the time at which John says Jesus was crucified (that is, at the sixth hour) is when the paschal lamb was being killed in the temple. The Last Supper was seen to be connected with the supreme sacrifice: Jesus, the offering for the sin of the world, the Lamb of God who takes away the sin of the world.

The Synoptic Gospels, however (Matthew, Mark and Luke), state quite clearly that the Last Supper took place on Passover itself, that the Passover meal was in remembrance of the Jesus who was crucified. For me, and indeed for many others, the Last Supper can be nothing more than a memorial, and the basis of this lies in Jesus's own words: 'Do this in remembrance of me'. What we see now is the development of the practice, and to my mind it has now become the exclusive thing it was never meant to be. My own belief is that to remember Jesus is all we are asked to do, that within the family relationship, in the sharing of the bread and the wine, we are simply recreating the conditions which bring us that much closer to God. 'Where two or three are gathered in my name, there am I in the midst.' God is there.

Since I see this as a remembrance service rather than an initiation and sacrificial ceremony, I see no reason why there should be an exclusion clause written into the invitation to join around the Lord's table. Even in the most reserved terms, the phrase 'Those who love the Lord Jesus Christ', creates a barrier which is sometimes insurmountable. Once I had a Church member who did not believe that participation in Holy Communion was necessary to salvation, and it is not if salvation is what is being offered or sought. He never stayed to celebrate, but, in making the invitation to those who love the Lord, I was implying that he left because he did not love the Lord, which in this case, and no doubt in others, was quite untrue. He knew he loved the Lord, I knew he loved the Lord, but the others were never quite sure. It is better, one would have thought, to extend the invitation to 'all whom the Lord loves', remembering in our heart of hearts that those who met around that first table were no better or worse than any of us who meet today: Peter, who denied his Lord, not once but three times; John and James who sought the best places in the kingdom; Thomas who doubted to the very end; and Judas the betrayer. Jesus did not say to them, 'Only those who love me can participate, can share in this supper'. Rather, his whole attitude reflected quite the reverse: 'You must stay in spite of what you are about to do or who you are, because I love you all.' He did not bid these misunderstanding helpmates to leave because of their shortcomings. No, he revealed to them the wonderful grace of God, operative still in spite of all their failures.

The need in the Church is to offer an open table to any who want to share. On one occasion there were fifty visitors because of an infant baptism. Communion followed, to which all were invited to stay. They did. I knew only the parents and child. We ran out of individual glasses, so those without wine, about eight, were invited to join the elders at the table and share what we had in the chalice. It was a moving and spiritual occasion for us all. No, we have not seen any of them back in Church since, but many came from a distance. They were all, however, received, invited to participate, to share our most intimate service. They had found a place. No, they had been offered a place and been denied nothing. One stranger, on leaving, was heard to say, 'I have never experienced anything like this in my whole life. They actually shared that which was most precious to them.'

Nothing is worth anything unless it is shared.

What can all this mean to these strangers? I do not know, but I know what it meant to us – that the Church was not exclusive, that we were prepared to share our worship without laying down conditions, that people can join us not because they are Christians, but because they are people, human souls with hearts that tick, created in God's image, made just a little lower than the angels and unique in a universe where no other human form exists as far as we know.

The question must be asked, 'Does this kind of invitation do any harm?' How can it? It can only cause people to ponder and perhaps come to some understanding that God does care in a world which can at times be very cold and uninviting, where we are in large measure depersonalised to a degree that is sometimes unbearable. If men, women and children are worth anything at all, and this is what the Bible is most consistent about from beginning to end, then the need is for us to show it. If it is the love of Christ we are expected to reveal, then it needs to be shown in every aspect of our living, including our most wonderful occasions around the Lord's table. We must not and cannot afford to keep the centre of our worship for our exclusive use, for in so doing we are returning to the Old Testament concept of the Jewish nation and its temple. All need to be able to venture beyond the communion rail, to share *at* the table, simply because the crucifixion and resurrection of Jesus make it possible.

But what about Paul's warning in the eleventh chapter of his letter to the Church in Corinth, which we are expected to use judging from our liturgical service manuals, words which, some would say, we must not leave out and which generally follow the words of the institution of the Lord's Supper and I quote: 'Therefore whoever eats this bread and drinks this cup of the Lord in an unfitting way is guilty of a sin against the body and blood of our Lord.'

We need to remind ourselves that these words come from Paul and not Jesus. They are part of Paul's developed thoughts on the subject, his interpretation of Holy Communion, and Paul was not thinking about us when he wrote, but rather of those to whom he was writing. Equally we do not possess the letters he was answering, and therefore do not know the problems (and there were many) with which he was dealing at that time. We can only deduce the situation which prompted his letter. Having just rebuked the recipients of his letter, who had. with their status and class distinctions, been dividing the Church, it could very well be that the man eating and drinking unworthily is he who for one reason or another is at variance with his fellow member.

But again we might ask, who is this Paul to talk like that, a man who actually excommunicated one of his fellow workers, whom Paul accused of being a deserter? The differences between them were so marked that they split company, never to work together again.

The truth is that the Church is not a true church when the art of sharing is forgotten. When people wish to keep things to themselves or their own circle, they are not even beginning to be Christian: the person who finds the greatest privilege not in jealously guarding the gifts of God in exclusiveness, but rather in giving them away.

The author remembers a young lady by the name of Barbara Nissman, an American of some acclaim in the musical world, who came to Britain and shared her musical talents via the piano with schools and factories, sharing with her listeners that which she loved most. She bubbled over with enthusiasm, eager to impart to the less initiated in the classical field some of the treasures of her profession – and the only cost was to herself.

We in the Church need to do just that. We have a treasure which we claim surpasses all other treasures. We have to share it, indeed we *must* share it, and without all the conditions and trappings which tend to confuse the whole issue of God's concern for each and every one. Let all come to the table who feel the need. It may not appeal to everyone but it will to some, and they are those who will stay.

A little girl sat in front of the author at a recent service which included the sharing of the bread and wine. She would have been about seven years of age. She was offered the bread but was somewhat puzzled and I think disappointed when she didn't get any wine (and it was non-alcoholic).

The matter was rectified when we shared the same glass. She was not left out. It is a form of rejection to pass people by, and many an ugly scar has been left on the minds of those who have been full of expectations and received nothing.

Chapter VI
Women and Ordination

Back in 1969/70, I was one of a number of Free Church ministers who met regularly at an ecumenical conference in Norwich to discuss possible ways and means of doing things together.

My view of the ecumenical situation at that time was that, having accomplished a great deal in joint services as well as the occasional inter-communion service, it was time that we took some additional steps at local level to further the work of the movement toward total Christian unity, something very close to my heart.

We had, as it were, come to a grinding halt, with the main stumbling block being the recognition of ministers in different denominations, a matter involving the question of the apostolic succession and bishops. It was not that the Free Churches did not recognise others, but that certain of the others did not recognise us, meaning that as far as church law was concerned we had a difficult task to enter the race, never mind getting a start. To resolve the problem of the men might not be too difficult, but the real thorn in the flesh was the recognition of our women ministers, whom we have in abundance.

That problem is still with us today.

The arguments for the refusal to ordain women in certain of the denominations are many and varied. Men, we are told, are the dominant figures in the Bible. Jesus was a man, as indeed were his disciples, and this is linked directly with the masculinity of God, who in my humble opinion is neither masculine nor feminine but neuter.

The Free Churches would take the view, in Britain anyway, that all are likely to be called to the ministry or priesthood, and that all are at liberty to and capable of responding to that call. This principle is based firmly upon the concept of the 'priesthood of all believers', implying that all believers have direct access to his or her Lord. It is understood that women are just as likely to respond to that call (and many do) as men, and that God is just as willing to receive them in a ministerial capacity. Women in the Free Churches have been so called and received since the turn of the present century. Such as are ordained have been known to make as good a job of it as men, some even better. Many have been appointed to high office with acclaim.

Of course it is not enough to make claims for the ordination of women without appropriate Biblical support, so it is proposed to show that the very evidence used by objectors in defence of their stand that women should not be included in the ministry is in fact evidence to substantiate the claim of women that they should be ordained, and that such claims are perfectly valid and should be upheld in God's name.

First it is submitted that those who find women ministers in the Church distasteful cannot really make a case for their exclusion, or rather it should perhaps be said that any case they make will not hold water.

What in fact is the objectors' case?

It is claimed that women have no place because Jesus did not call women to be his disciples. The truth is that there is no Scriptural foundation for the belief that Jesus preferred to call men. Indeed, we do not know whether women *were* called although it is unlikely, for the very simple reason that Jesus was well aware that the women of his day would have been unable to perform the task which a disciple was expected to do, not because they could not but because they would not be allowed. Jesus knew, as indeed his contemporaries knew, that any such call would be quite contrary to custom. Not that Jesus was a slave of custom, but the notion of women's inferiority was the order of the day and the generally accepted norm. We only have to read some of the New Testament letters to see how women were regarded, even by those who claimed to be most devout.

'Women should learn in silence,' says Paul. 'I do not allow women to teach or have authority over men. They must be quiet. For Adam was created first and then Eve.'

Paul goes on to accuse women of having broken the law in the first place, reflecting a general degradation of women, cultivated no doubt from his knowledge of the Old Testament. Such inferiority disqualified women from any kind of office, and was inferred from Eve's creation and her connivance with the serpent in the Garden of Eden.

Paul's first letter to the Corinthians reiterates the same view: 'It is a disgraceful thing for women to speak at a church meeting'. And again, in the first fourteen verses of Chapter Eleven. This puts woman, in Paul's view, right in the place she obviously belongs – under the authority of men.

Jesus was not unaware of the way in which women were treated, but he recognised that the women of his day would not have been able to carry out the task He had in mind, simply because they were concerned primarily with the domestic rather than the religious. The man was the dominant factor in the family, and it was the man who would be most likely to be able to follow Jesus's commands, the men who could put up with the conditions which Jesus expected would arise as a result of his ministry.

Most of what is claimed by those who would see only men in the role of a priest finds support from Paul in the passages already quoted, but, far from supporting a claim in the twentieth century, they merely point out, in no uncertain terms, why Jesus did not choose women. If He had He would have been laughed to scorn. It was quite unthinkable, according to Jewish law and custom, that women should claim any kind of equality with men, and to this end they were segregated. They had been created out of Adam's rib (Genesis 2), they were vastly inferior to men, they were the 'helpmeet' of man, created for man's sake. Women were things. It was only the 'loose' women or the poor women who were seen about in the streets. To teach the law to women was 'to cast pearls before swine'. Among the plagues of the world were included 'the talkative and imaginative widow, and the virgin who wastes her time in prayers'. It was forbidden to speak to a woman in the street; one could not ask a service of or salute a woman. Their inferiority disqualified them from any kind of position in the community. They were expected to keep their proper place, the veil being the sign of their subjection and acting as a protection for their modesty and chastity. Respectable women would not have been seen without it.

In the early Church there was little change: Paul's letters were written against both a Greek and Jewish background where generally women had a low position. They were, for instance, at the disposal of their father and husband. They were forbidden to learn the law or participate in synagogue worship, and were, on occasions, shut away where they could not be seen. They came to the synagogue to hear, to listen and were forbidden to read at the service, for this would result in a 'lessening of the honour of the congregation'. They were not allowed to teach in school, not even the youngest classes. Respectable women led a confined life in their own quarters and the only unrelated male allowed to see them was their husband. A Jewish woman did not appear in front of strangers for meals, never walked the streets alone, and never attended or took part in any public assembly. It is said that if any woman had taken an active speaking or teaching role, the Church would have gained the reputation of being a haven for loose women.

In the light then of such circumstances surrounding the female population, is it likely that Jesus would have chosen any to be his disciples? To have done so at that time would have served no useful purpose, and would have done nothing to help his cause. Added to that, a great deal of unnecessary scorn would have been heaped upon his head and made him a laughing stock. No one would have given their words or actions a passing thought. Women disciples would at that time have been nothing but a disastrous choice, not because Jesus did not want them but because he knew the customs of the day and had no desire to bring derision upon anyone, let alone the women.

Paul, in his ministry, was unable to rise above the ideas with which he had grown up, hence his references to women in his letters. It was Sophocles who said that 'it is silence that confers grace upon a woman', but it is unlikely that Paul wished them to keep silent in order that more grace might be forthcoming, but rather that, in line with his own upbringing, women were simply non-starters in the race.

That men exclusively were chosen as Jesus's disciples was surely because they were most likely to prove the best ambassadors of the Word at that time. They were free as women were not free, they were respected where women were not, and the choice of women to carry the banner for the Jesus campaign would have left it in tatters. Not that the men did much better, but it was the best possible approach for the battle that lay ahead.

It has to be said, however, that with increasing understanding in the early Church of this comparatively new concept of equality which Jesus encouraged as far as possible, the place of women began to improve, and has continued to do so ever since, although many women in the world still have, unfortunately, to take a back seat. Mrs Golda Meir would seem to be the exception rather than the rule in

Israel. Jesus's ministry was the beginning of what has now become full recognition of equal rights, and it would appear quite wrong to suggest in our own time that there is no place for women in the ministry of the Church. If Jesus were to return today, he would no doubt be extremely happy about the marked increase of women participating in the affairs of the Church and certainly pleased about the positive results of a movement begun during those early Galilean days. It is doubtful whether he would have any hesitation at all in choosing a mixed team to help fulfil his task, perhaps even wholly female in the light of the knowledge that men have not done too well during the last two thousand years.

The recent outcome of the vote at the Anglican Synod must be applauded, but one would guess that it is not the end of the matter. To get it through Parliament will be a major task, but hopes remain high.

The dirty deed is done and most if not all of the women deacons in the Church of England have now achieved their goal. We wonder what all the fuss was about. While there is still some opposition, where women applicants for posts will not be entertained, it is to their credit that women are doing a first-class job in appointments where they have every right to be.

But they are not a first in this field. The first woman ordained into the ministry of the Church was in the then Congregational Church in 1910, and that with the least of fuss.

Chapter VII
Death and the Dying

I am a part-time hospital chaplain and have been for the last fourteen years, and find that the ministry of the Church to the dying is not as good as it should be, mainly because the physical and social needs of the patient are, in the main, attended to by the state. Spiritual needs comes a long way down on the list. My connection with hospitals has, albeit in the same place, opened my eyes about attitudes within the hospital environment. Some may find their experiences different from mine, but, judging from some of the comments made at various chaplains' conferences, they are similar in many respects.

For instance, information about patients is strictly limited. Indeed one could go as far as to say it is practically non-existent. I say practically, because of the odd occasion when one manages to make a crack in the stonewall position invariably maintained by the staff. 'Are you a relative?' is the question. If not, the reply is that it is up to the patient to provide religious information. Everything comes under the cloak of confidentiality in spite of the fact that chaplains are on the staff, and that the word 'confidentiality' means more to us than anything else. Sisters on the wards are helpful, and we are normally allowed to wander around at any odd time of the day or night, which is in effect an entitlement, but sometimes regarded with suspicion as though we were intruders. What is paramount is that the patient's condition must remain a secret. When a person is 'past the post', or has 'slipped his cable' as we often say in naval language, then and only then should our interest be aroused. What a lot of nonsense that is.

Such a situation may have arisen simply because we in the Church have not dug in our heels. Doctors can be most uncooperative, especially if they are not religiously minded. Invariably all we want to know is whether the patient is on the mend or otherwise. It helps in assessing what one is likely to say. That is important for any who have to minister to the sick. Many of the folks who are unfortunate enough to become hospital patients are church folk – indeed there are few who have no religious denomination at all – and they look to the chaplain or their own minister for a word from the Lord and especially a word of comfort. It is utterly useless, of course, to give the impression that all is well when one is aware of a deteriorating condition. 'Don't worry, lass, you'll be out in a couple of days.' And so she is – in a coffin. Miracles do happen, but the choice of words can be extremely difficult when one does not know how the invalid is doing. In such a situation a great deal of irreparable damage can be done. I have met it more than once, when someone has been known to say the wrong thing.

This, however, for me, is not the main difficulty. It is the death that bothers me, and the subsequent effect on the close relatives – the mums, dads, wives, husbands, daughters, sons, and the children – plus all the others who are affected by the loss. Relatives are often caught up in the haunting tales of hell's destruction, and have to face the fact that a great deal of our hymns, together with much that we are asked to read at funeral services, reflect fearful thoughts of going to the wrong place (if place is the right word). People ought to come to church to allay such fears, but the truth is that such fears often keep people away. Of course there is a great deal in Scripture that marks delineation, but funerals are not the best time for any theological views about heaven and hell, and in any case we are not those who will decide the deceased ultimate destination. Our hope surely, if we are to reflect the kind of love for our neighbour which Jesus advocates, is that we should all arrive at the same place. It is up to us to do the best we can, to offer people the assurance of their rightful place within the compass of God's kingdom, leaving any thoughts of reward or punishments firmly out of sight.

The procedures for the disposal of the body can be so impersonal that it can bring one to tears. Some folk cope very well, but the majority do not. I have few complaints about the funeral directors, although I have met some who are totally insensitive to the needs of the next of kin. Nor have I any criticism of the staff of crematoria, although I hate those press button affairs wholly monitored from a single console. They reflect an impersonality which at times is beyond belief. Equally the symbolism at crematoria is totally out of keeping with the kind of hopes we have.

It may be that some do not notice, perhaps they are too sad to care, but my experience of some of the symbolism throughout the country leaves much to be desired, indicating that those who design the buildings have failed to communicate with those who actually perform the ceremonies. To be burned up in an oven is psychologically unsound, for it resembles a vision of hellfire, where no one has any desire to go. To descend in a catafalque is again, symbolic of hell, all of which is quite contrary to everything we are trying to say to people, Christian or otherwise, who cannot bring themselves to believe that death is the end? One place sent the coffin off at speed, through what one supposed to be the pearly gates, not into the shining light of the heavenly kingdom but the total darkness of hell, all of which brought forth an unholy scream from the next of kin. Crematoria need to be redesigned, and those still to be built need to reflect the hope of the Christian faith, using symbolism which is in keeping with the gospel message of a loving Father.

This of course is not always an easy thing to do, because such facilities have to be offered to everybody, those of all religious faiths and of none. For those who profess nothing then, whether the coffin goes up or down or across, whether it ends up in a fiery furnace to be consumed does not really matter; but it can be distressing for those who associate going down and fire with hell, in spite of the assurances offered by those of us who do not happen to preach in these terms.

Equally one ought to see these occasions as opportunities for creative relationships where one can express, without any strings, a genuine tenderness and concern which reflects the caring attitude of the Church. For this reason alone the Church needs, on the majority of occasions, to replace the more stereotyped service with something more simple, something more personal and related to the needs of the mourners. Much of what is set down to be said at funeral services is wholly ecclesiastical and in the main alien and meaningless. Often it is couched in a phraseology which, as well as being flowery, has nothing to really say to the mourners. Many people, including the deceased and the relations, have no direct connection with the Church, but are nominally one thing or the other and are unfamiliar with the jargon of the standard religious service. I have known the whole of the Fifteenth Chapter of 1 Corinthians to be read during a service, which, to the uninitiated, must have sounded like a coded message of World War II vintage, leaving them completely out of their depth.

Often many families reside a long way from the crematorium, and it is difficult to know anything about the deceased's background. It is therefore important that they find something in the service which conveys the love and care of God. As far as funerals are concerned, I happen to be a universalist and firmly believe that the resurrection is for all or it is for nobody. I cannot understand a loving God who is anything else but loving. The kind of mansion we receive when we finally depart henceforth is not for us to determine, but a mansion there will be. It is not for us to condemn, or indeed judge, but to assure.

Added to that, local authorities seem to bypass the Church as though there were no alternatives to going to a crematorium for the service. It may very well be the Church's fault that this is so, saying as they often do, that only those connected with the Church are entitled, so to speak, to use its facilities; but, generally speaking, the self-same service is the norm, as per the book of words, at the crematorium, so there would appear to be little difference. Crematoria were never built for religious services but primarily for the disposal of bodies, and religious services would be better held in church if people were given the opportunity. People think that because they do not go to church they have no business to ask for its services when someone dies. I believe that the Church ought to open its doors to all, where the facilities for the spiritual needs of the mourners can be met, and equally the hope of resurrection, which most people in my experience seem to hang on to, even though they do not express it in any traditionally worshipful way. This ought be offered as an alternative, and the Church ought to cooperate in the fullest possible way. Crematoria should be used for committals only.

Certainly clergy are used where necessary in the crematorium service, but it would seem more fitting for the coffin to be left in the church for removal to the crematorium after the bereaved have gone home. For relatives to accompany the cortège to the crematorium, and there to witness the finality (though some would choose no doubt to see things through to the bitter end) of either a drawn curtain or a descending catafalque can be depressing. Worse, however, is to see the remains of the previous lifeless soul going up in smoke.

If we were all practising Christians there would be no problem, for funerals would be seen, amidst the obvious sorrow of losing a loved one, as a joyful occasion of blessing instead of punishment, but while people still hang on to the old concepts of hellfire for the unsaved, and this, unfortunately, is perpetuated in our own time, there is a need to remove the symbolism which, in large measure encourages such thinking in order that we might better express the basic truth that God is light and in him there is no darkness at all.

In contrast with other aspects of the Christian faith, I find that many denominations are inconsistent when it comes to the burial or cremation of the dead. One finds it difficult to understand an attitude which on the one hand denies Christian baptism and Christian marriage unless there are a great deal of strings attached while on the other will offer Christian burial to any Tom, Dick or Mary. Why are the same principles not applied when people are alive rather than waiting till they are dead and gone? What credentials does the dead person have which others, who at times seek the Church's assistance for other services, have not? Not only is it inconsistent but it is totally out of keeping with the grace and love of God, and indeed with the kind of compassionate spirit shown by Christ in his ministry and which was offered to all and not just a select few. It is a judgement which is totally invalid.

There are many criticisms from the community at large regarding the disposal of our nearest and dearest. A recent survey revealed that: The crematorium is known as the place 'for the disposal of bodies'; 'a place like a sausage machine.'

Services in a church would do something to dispel these ideas.

The services have been described as 'above our heads', 'all pretty meaningless', 'all so cold with no personal involvement'.

Simple down-to-earth services without too much theological jargon or even Scripture readings (I dispensed with those years ago; quotations, yes) must take the place of the stereotyped order, if we are to make any sense of dying at all, if we are to show that we have some concern for the people involved, even if it is only for that brief spell which can mean so much (or so little) at a time of distress.

'A medieval service... like a black comedy compared with Monty Python... all too mechanical to be personal.'

A change in the symbolism is a must if we are to retain crematoria in their present form. Otherwise there must be a change of venue.

After all if the service is in the church, one does not *have* to go to the committal. People ought to be persuaded to go home after the service. For myself, no two services are alike, primarily because the passing of John Smith is unique to the Smith family and not to the Jones family who were here half an hour before.

And what form should the service take? Let the family have anything they like. Their own choice of music – instead of a few hymns from which to choose, and which often they do not know – readings of their own choice, and perhaps prayers as well. 'Can I have *I'll Take You Home Again Kathleen*, or Glen Miller?' And why not? I say, why not? I am sure the good Lord will accept anything offered in the right spirit.

Chapter VIII
By What Authority

The need here is to remind readers that in the foregoing chapters the concern is not for those already committed to the Church or indeed, those who are familiar with the standards and principles in the practice of the Christian faith, but rather with those who go about ignorant of these issues, ignorant in the main through no fault of their own.

It may be that their parents have never been associated with the Church or perhaps discontinued going for one reason or another at a very young age. It may also be that religious education for them was a non-starter insofar as the majority of schools today do not show any real interest in the understanding of the Christian faith. It is just one among others, and often comes low on the priority list especially if the headteacher is anti, as many are.

Indeed, many see the religious clauses of the 1944 Education Act as an imposition on the teaching profession. There may be dozens of reasons why folks do not link baptism and marriage with living standards, or why they still hold antediluvian concepts about the Church, kindled and often fuelled no doubt by old wives' tales, and often by the image of the Church they see. Some have forgotten that the Church exists and find no need for its services, even for the passing away of relatives and friends.

Some would argue that the image they see is not a true one, distorted by their lack of knowledge and understanding of what the Church is really meant to be, but nevertheless this image is likely to remain until it is changed, and that does not come about by expecting such folk to make lifelong commitments at the drop of a hat, meaning after two or three or even twelve weeks of initiation training. The disciples had been with Jesus for three years and at the end of it all were still ignorant about the meaning of many aspects of his ministry.

We are concerned with people who have little idea if any, of what the Church is all about, of what the Bible is all about, and that in spite of its being a bestseller. They have little idea of how much community work is done by the Church, or what we do when we get into what some would describe as 'our holy huddle' on a Sunday. Of course there are plenty of books on the subject, but we find it a tough job even to get our church-going folk to read them. We had an exercise some years ago about unity and produced what was described as 'The Ten Propositions' for discussion in the Churches. A year after their publication, when asked how they were coping with the task, one colleague was known to ask, 'What are they?'

When asking the man in the street about such an issue, one is met with a blank look. Even the present debate in the Church of England regarding the ordination of women, publicised as it has been on TV, is an unknown quantity. It is just not part of their scene, but when it comes to their child being baptised or married then it is very much their scene because this involves *their* family. It comes right into their home, and that is where we have to start, from square one. Many such people are not even familiar with the word 'hymn', let alone what it means to confess Christ as Lord. While many can tell you where the local pub is, when asked about the church, and especially the United Reformed Church, they are quite unaware of the name, never mind the location, and they nearly fall over when you suggest that it might just be that building across the road: 'Well then, that is a surprise! You know, I have lived here for ten years and never noticed that before. I thought it had something to do with the local council.' And this in spite of a large noticeboard with the name written large for all to see.

But it is no more or less like the question put to me by a 'stranger' to the town: 'Can you tell me please where I can find Canby House? It is where the local camera club meets.' I cannot say because I have never been there and the need for me to go has never arisen. A church is simply a building, the same as the local branch of the post office is a building. We have to use the post office because we need stamps and to post letters, but the church is never visited because there is nothing in it we need, nor does it offer anything we want; that is until the baby arrives or the daughter or son is to be married, and often because Mum or Dad says so or because their friend had theirs done. That is as good a reason as any.

Is there any reason, therefore, why such requests should not be met? These are common folk just like ourselves, for whom Jesus died and for whom He equally has high hopes, people who seldom see the inside of a church ('I never knew it was like this. Isn't it lovely?') and who have little idea about what is done or how people behave once inside. Once upon a time the church was full of children. Sadly the attendance of children is falling off and has been for many years. All the more reason, then, to start where they are, meeting their individual needs and sharing some of their time, their hopes and their fears, which they always seem ready to do.

And what more authority do we need than that of Jesus himself? He met the needs of people without condition, without awkward questions, without asking for a history of their past life, and that in spite of their lack of faith, and in direct opposition to the authorities of his day who said that he was not allowed to do things on certain days, and also contrary to the common Church approach that it needs a public profession of faith before anything can be done.

For this reason alone the New Testament for the beginner must be in large measure a non-starter. We are dealing as far as the Christian faith is concerned, and with all due respect, with three and four year olds. Just as if I want to learn how to use this word processor I have to start at the beginning, it is the same for any new venture, and the religious life is indeed a new venture, as the writer found out many moons ago.

Paul, in his letter to the Church in Corinth, has this to say (and I don't always agree with his pontifications): 'As a matter of fact my brothers, I could not talk to you as I talk to people who have the Spirit; I had to talk to you as though you belonged to this world as children in the faith, I had to feed you with milk, not with solid food, because you were not ready...'

If was true of the new converts, how much more is it true for the uncommitted? There is a great need to see the necessity for spoon-feeding, even to the extent that the Bible is not even mentioned. To talk about what Jesus did and continues to do is an indication of personal knowledge of him, but even this needs a cautious approach depending very much on how the situation develops.

A young lady asked me to call at her home. She was about twenty-one years of age and had been married (in a register office) about two years ago. She wanted her new baby christened. Neither she nor her husband had ever been to church before, apart from the fact that he had gone to a Sunday School outing once.

'What do we do?' was the question. Now, to suggest that they go through a long course of instruction in order that they might be able to respond to the questions positively (as per the book) was lunacy of the highest order. We are, after all, dealing with the baby and not the parents. The service was arranged, but not in the church, in her house because the lady in question suffered from a crowd phobia, which her husband confirmed. 'And what about the water?' she asked, and was rather taken aback when I suggested that she get some from the kitchen tap. She had some notion that we shipped it in from Jerusalem or had a special brand locked away in the church safe. She asked if she could be done at the same time, and frowned when I mentioned that this could be dealt with at another time.

On a Sunday afternoon a few weeks later there were twenty-seven people in the house, twenty-three of whom had never been in church before. 'And they are never likely to be!' someone cried. Well, perhaps not, but this simple service in someone's home seemed to me to be ministry at its best. Added to that, Mum was baptised at the same time. The Church was seen to minister to that family's needs, without strings, without barriers, without arm twisting and indeed without specific promises that to all intents and purposes would never be kept, very much as my parents never kept theirs.

No, these folks do not come to church, but I know that I can walk through their door at any time and be welcomed as a friend, and as a representative of God. The seed has been sown, but now it needs nourishing if it is to grow, and that is the Church's task. It could be, however, that someone some day will neglect their pastoral duties because this particular family does not belong, and the young plant will die. That is a chance we have to take. The onus, however, is not on the family, but upon us – the gardeners who planted the seed. If the seed is nourished it will stand every chance of growing. If not it will surely perish.

For such folk, the place to start is with Jesus and his work, his concern for the lost sheep – not to imply at this stage or at any other for that matter that they are lost, but simply to talk about what Jesus did in similar circumstances to their own. *That* they will understand, and that is all they need to understand at that point in their family affairs. The story in the Acts of the Apostles might help, but it is basically about the activities of the early Church. It is early Church history which, in the early stages of creative relationships, does not really matter. Again Paul's letters are written to growing communities with, as it were, religious labour pains, offering directives, encouragement, instruction and oftimes a rebuke for mistakes already committed. They were written for those who in some measure understood what was happening in the life of the community, people who, being Jews of the Diaspora, believed in God anyway, together with Gentiles who were seeking a freedom which seemed to be offered in the Gospel message, a faith among many faiths, which was new and refreshing, but about which they were largely ignorant.

Jesus talked with the woman at the well. The Samaritans, although of the same stock, were long-standing enemies of the Jews. Indeed it was forbidden for a Jew even to look at a woman, never mind talk to her. But Jesus chose to indulge in conversation. And what kind of woman was she, one might ask? Married five times over and living with a man who was not her husband. Jesus did not offer her living water on condition that she changed her wicked ways and started going to church. Indeed not. He offered it to her as she was. There is no record of what she did except tell her friends, and it was the result of His conversation with this woman that brought others to him, who believed. Generally, in Jesus's healing ministry, the work was carried out without question or judgement. The sick, the maimed and the blind all came to him and He refused none. Of the ten lepers He cured, only one came back to say thanks and he was a Samaritan. Jesus was surrounded with the insistent demands of human need, and, selfless and uncomplaining, and with a divine generosity, He met them all. So long as there was a soul in need, there was no rest for Jesus. These words are not mine, but from the pen of the late Professor William Barclay of Glasgow University commenting on Matthew, Chapter Eight.

'If you want to heal me, you can,' said the leper. And Jesus said, 'I do.' And He did. Yes, the leper was asked to go and see a priest, but there is no record of his having done so. All the references in the Sermon on the Mount point to the unique worth of humankind: 'Will God not be able the more to clothe you?'; 'Do not judge'; 'Look at the log in your own eye, then go and make friends with your brother'; 'Ask and you will receive; knock and the door will be opened; seek and you will find'; 'For *everyone* who asks will receive'; 'The very hairs of your head are numbered'. Jesus saw the crowds, who came with all sorts of motives, many of them selfish. He was used, but he had pity for they were worried and helpless, like sheep without a shepherd.

Where, one might ask, does the healing, and the shepherding process begin? How do we start? Surely baptising the baby and marrying the divorced can be and often is the beginning of the healing process, perhaps a sign to the uninitiated that God really cares for them.

Jesus called the twelve disciples, who as far as we are aware were not baptised, not even known to have made any formal declaration of faith at the outset, only after they had been with Jesus for some considerable time. And what is it that He asked them to do? Heal the sick, raise the dead, make the leper clean and drive out the demons.

'You', said Jesus, 'have received without paying, so give without being paid.'

In other words what they had received had been given freely, without condition and without price. This does not of course mean that there was no price to pay, but that any price forthcoming had to come as a freely willed offering - a price willingly given and not wrung out of those who needed help most.

There is a great deal of talk (and generally among Church folk) that people use the Church for their own ends. There are those who take advantage of the facilities to marry in church because it is the right style. But is this really the case? After all, people do pay and often handsomely, for the services of the Church, which is seldom out of pocket. There have been times when I have offered to do the whole thing free of charge if the couple are a bit hard-up, as sometimes they are. It has never yet been the case, but come in your bare feet and on your bicycles if you wish and you will get exactly the same care and consideration as anyone else. In any case, why Christian marriage only for the Christian? Are we in fact saying that the uncommitted bride or groom do not mean what they say when they make their vows before God? The promise, as I understand it, is to be a loving and dutiful husband or wife till death intervenes, and I have yet to come across those who do not want that at the time in question. They do not, in the ceremony, have to promise to come to church regularly or even now and again, or, for that matter, make any public profession of faith.

What we are saying in the Church is that there are two kinds of marriage, one which is legal and done through the registrar and another, also legal but designed especially for the Christian. I have always thought that marriage in church was a ceremony conducted for those who desired that God should be involved, and not specifically for Christians. This smacks so much of the closed shop attitude that one begins to wonder why one should want to get married in church at all. Often the attitude is, 'If you are uncommitted and unlikely to become so, then we have no time for you here, unless of course you are prepared to conform.' It is strange that often the couple are not given a little time, do not get the chance to become committed. They are told immediately no chance.

As far as being used is concerned, there is every reason to believe that the majority of Jesus's contemporaries used him to their advantage. Where were they, one might ask, when he was nailed to the cross? The truth is that, like the disciples, they scampered up the road. There must have been dozens, nay hundreds of folks who had been baptised and healed during Jesus's brief ministry, so where did they go when the crunch came? Up the road without a trace, hanging about in the background, afraid to speak their minds for fear of ending up like the man they had promised to follow, if indeed that is what baptism and healing meant.

Yes, Jesus was used all right, but did he not say that he had come to serve and not to judge, that he had come to heal the broken heart and soul and not condemn?

'Father forgive them.' Forgive whom? Not simply Herod and Pilate and Peter and Judas and the jeering crowd, but all of those who had anything to do with this man of God: the healed; the baptised; the sinners; the publicans; the chief priests; the wine bibbers; the disciples, who were as much in need of forgiveness as the rest; and, last but not least, those who had nothing at all. Yes, he was used, right to the very end, but he did not appear to mind that. And he is being used now, in ways that bear no relation to the Gospel he practised and preached. He is being used as a cloak, an umbrella, for those who would seek to impose conditions upon the souls who need the love of God most of all: 'we can do nothing unless...'; 'our principles do not allow us to do that...'; 'the rules forbid us to get involved'.

I like to think that I belong to an organisation where people are free to come and go as they please, where there is a constant open door for anyone who cares to come in, where you do not have to acquire references or nominators; unlike a particular member of a political party who said, 'We are choosy whom we have here. You have to be recommended, you know.'

I would trust that the Church sees the human soul in a different light, but, unfortunately, it is chained in many ways to its rules and regulations which, in the end, will be its ruin.

Certainly there are instances where Jesus met people's needs and this led to gratitude and ultimately discipleship. Such an instance we find in the healing of blind Bartimaus, and this was certainly a time of rejoicing, but the whole life of Jesus seems, to me, to be the classic example of the Parable of the Sower. He sowed the seed, and some fell on stony ground and rocky ground, among the tares and on the good ground. It did not all take root and grow, as Jesus's ministry clearly shows, and we are not to know who will go selfishly away or turn in grateful response. It is as well that we do not, otherwise we might be tempted to work only for those whom we know are going to see the light. That is not how Jesus worked. He did what was necessary for them all.

Christianity began with a personal reaction to a Jesus who met their particular need at a particular moment, with an instinctive feeling that God had done something for them; and in the eyes of the common folk of our own time the Church is seen to represent God and they see God often in the way the Church responds to their needs. If the Church refuses to do that, which in the end cannot do anyone any harm – to baptise, marry, or bury – but which in the last analysis brings some kind of joy and happiness into their lives, then we do nothing but create barriers between God and his people.

When Jesus talked about the weary and heavy-laden coming to him for rest, he was talking about the burden of the law of his day. If it comes between God and his people, then it must graciously, but nevertheless effectively, be set aside. The law of the Church has in large measure become a burden around her neck, and many have expressed the view that they would gladly see it left in the pages of antiquity where it originated, a Word for its time but certainly not for the twentieth century.

Yes, indeed we have a story of the temptations of Jesus, about the short cuts to the hearts of men and women which Jesus quite rightly refused to accept by resorting to the spectacular, to the gimmick - but this is not what we are being asked to do. It may rightly be said that to baptise all children, to marry divorcé(e)s and the non-committed in church may undermine the authority of the Church, but is it not also the case that it may, among other things, emphasise the willingness of God to love and receive people just as they are? To offer these services without condition will surely not negate or indeed diminish the importance of baptism or of marriage, for they are done believing wholeheartedly that this is what God would have us do. Even if those whom we have served never show their face inside a church, if we never see them again, as often happens, surely they will be happy in the knowledge that for once in their lifetime they have had an experience of God at work in their family affairs, that they invited him and he did not refuse the invitation.

The Church is often accused of keeping the Good News to itself, strictly for those inside, that marriage and baptism are strictly for the privileged few. If this is not a 'closed shop' attitude, then we are deluding ourselves, and there is no earthly use in talking about such things as being against the common folk within a union framework, if we ourselves are guilty of the same practices.

To carry out in practice what has been said in these pages might seem like throwing principle to the winds, but this is not in fact the case. It is utterly useless to try and impose rules upon other people, for, in the end, the only rules that matter are those one applies to oneself. Those we will keep. Our own creed is the one that is most important of all. My standards remain the same because I have accepted them for myself. I believe that infant baptism is a means of grace, just as I believe that marriage in church is. I believe that the Church must practise what she preaches when she says that all men are equal in the sight of God, that they all have the same importance, meaning that they all, saint and sinner alike, should be treated in the same way. It seems, however, that most of the benefits of the Church are available only to those who conform. Where does the concept of sharing come in when we are dealing with the grace of God? In reality, his grace is not ours to share, to dispense to those only whom we think worthy of it. Grace is free and on offer without charge: 'Having freely received... freely give.'

The communion table, another centre of controversy among denominations, is something which I see as a means of sharing God's grace. The table has become exclusive to the initiated, a Calvinistic concept which has no place in modern Church life. The reason is a simple one. We need to take stock of those who sat around that first table: Peter, who denied his Lord not once but three times, and after all his assurances that he would do otherwise; Thomas, who doubted from the very beginning; John and James, selfish in the extreme, asking to be Jesus's chief ministers of state; Judas the betrayer. Jesus did not turn any of them away, but rather had the same hopes for all, that through sharing a simple meal they might recognise what he was doing, not only for them, but for all mankind, that they might know the love of God in their hearts.

To share the bread and wine with a stranger or the uncommitted can be no bad thing if in that sharing they, and we, see and feel something of the influence of the presence of Christ. It is a time of witness, and it is in keeping these things to ourselves that we become very much like those other bodies who revel in their initiation ceremonies where access for the ordinary man in the street becomes impossible. It is in this kind of selfishness that we, as a Church, stand condemned, when we have so much we can share with those who seek on occasion to ask or knock on our door.

I like to believe that I belong to a society or, preferably, a fellowship with the largest membership in the world, where people are not only free to come, but equally free to go if they choose – where *we* do not commit them but they commit themselves. Our task is to plant the seed of faith and help it to grow. That is as much as we are responsible for, and we should be at liberty to do it as the occasion arises without being tied to rules and regulations which, in the main, do not, and cannot, apply to anyone outside the Church.

To deny the love of God to anyone is to be guilty of restrictive practice, the closed shop attitude, discrimination, exclusiveness and, more than that, self-righteousness of the highest order – the sin which finally brought the Jews to their knees in AD 70.

Chapter IX
Beyond the Now

Having passed a great deal of comment about some of the things that bother me in Church life, I close with a simple yet what must be something of a controversial statement – that the Church seems in large measure to have lost her way.

Somehow she has missed the point, very much like the Old Testament Jews missed the point.

I believe that the Holy Spirit is guiding us (or is it me in my old age who is misguided?), as indeed it guided others before us, to see something unique in the person of Jesus, towards a new vision, not only of the Church but a new vision of God himself.

Many years ago a gentleman by the name of J.B. Phillips wrote, among other things, a book with the title *Your God is Too Small*, suggesting that we seek to pigeonhole God into our own particular hole or mould. He was saying that God was and is much greater, more generous, more concerned, more loving and more forgiving than we can ever understand.

I am sure that he is right, but it appears as if the Church has ignored or maybe has just not recognised the importance of that message. Perhaps the book has not been altogether highly regarded or even read for that matter, but that cannot be said of the Gospels. Anyone who claims to be either a Jew or a Christian must be conversant with the Bible. Indeed many who do not claim to be either of these religious persuasions have a fair knowledge of the Bible, and have scrutinised its contents at length. I say this because we are constantly faced with messages of one shape or another, reflecting what different writers understand to be the crux of the life and teaching of this man Jesus and of the Church who claims him as her Lord.

One such message was contained in another more recent publication, entitled *The Other Side of 1984*, wherein the writer asks some pertinent questions of the Churches, stating that the accepted framework of understanding in all the denominations, meaning those under the umbrella of orthodoxy, has become inadequate, and calls for a new framework which will recognise that, in addition to Western cultures, there are other frameworks with which we have to be concerned.

It is said that when one lives within a completely different culture and learns a new language one discovers other ways of grasping experience and coping with life and all it means. One discovers, says the writer, that things are seen differently through different spectacles.

It would appear that the writer took rather a long time to find out that basic truth, which, for one who has been around a bit, is quite self-evident. It was again the late Professor William Barclay who said that if you want to understand the other person, you need to see life through his or her eyes, or, to put it another way, get right inside their skin; meaning, of course, that for a time you need to become one of them.

Our writer goes on to say that it is about time we began to talk to others in this world who happen, through no fault of their own, to live inside another culture, and continues by using illustrations from his experience in India. He was put out of action for a while due to an accident with a local bus, and when visited in hospital by an Indian pastor was told that his accident was 'the will of God'. The Hindu on the other hand would claim that in karma the reason for his predicament was simply that the results of his actions in a previous life had caught up with him. Other cultures might claim that the hospitalisation was because his enemies had laid a curse on him. To say that the accident happened because some clown had failed to service the brakes properly would be, for those other cultures, no explanation at all.

So it is important that some kind of dialogue should take place among all these different frameworks, so that some common ground might be found whereby we might come to understand anew the intricate workings of Almighty God, and what the writer of *The Other Side of 1984* would suggest as the common denominator: the source of the principles which ought to govern the lives of individuals and societies, is, would you believe, the Bible, which he sees as the basis of ultimate hope and the salvation of all these different kinds of folk spread all over the world.

The need, however, is to consider those other cultures which are in essence dominated by other living faiths, those with whom we are encouraged to discuss the possibilities of a better understanding, and, if we look close enough, we will find that in places like Sri Lanka, there is constant pressure to return to the Buddhist dharma as the basis of society, while in many Muslim countries there are relentless attempts to reorganise society on the basis of the Koran. Equally there is increasing pressure in India to make Hinduism the official religion of society as a whole.

So it would seem that the problem is essentially with the source from which these basic principles of living should be drawn; and that is to say nothing of those countries which make up at least half the population of the world, who do not accept any of the aforementioned sources.

In a Buddhist-Hindu-Muslim nation it is extremely doubtful whether replacing their scriptures with the Bible can even be contemplated, any more than we in the Western world might consider replacing the Bible with, say, the Koran. The recent Salman Rushdie affair is proof of that. Some would claim that this indicates the urgent need for mission, so that other faiths might be persuaded, if not converted, into accepting Biblical principles. This writer's missionary activities in Malaysia were strictly curtailed with the threat of decapitation for even venturing to talk about the Christian faith. Any effort to convert or even persuade seem to border on the implication that these other faiths have nothing to offer. Also it would seem to deny, in a quite unidentifiable way, that, running parallel with the Biblical concept of man, there run other ways of organising life which hold just as lofty principles, some of which were present long before the earliest Biblical history.

Again it should always be taken into account, as many have rightly held, that in the course of any discussions or dialogue, no one has the right to assume that all the truth is theirs, and this should be a warning to those of us who get involved when we sometimes tend to believe that the truths we proclaim are so secure that there is no real danger in being challenged. The fact that the Churches, in Britain at least, are not so well supported as they once were clearly indicates that much of what we say *is* being challenged every day of the week. We only have to talk to those who do not enter our doors to find out. So where does that leave us in this year of grace?

My own understanding, which has arisen out of many difficult experiences of life, and indeed out of what the Old and New Testament has to say to us in our time, is that the framework suggested is still far too small even if there was some remote possibility of its being accepted, which in my view there is not.

We talk, we sing, we pray about God's world, then get on to advocate conversation among these frameworks, leaving out the only framework that matters and for which God exists. Jesus did not talk about frameworks: he spoke about God's world. He pointed beyond himself to the Father, humanity's father, and for this reason there is an urgent need to get away from the framework idea unless it is a framework which embraces all of mankind. It is also noted that while we are encouraged to converse with other faiths, there is little or no indication about conversations with those who have no faith at all and who make up just as many souls, for whom Jesus also gave his life, and about whom God is equally concerned. If we need a common denominator, here it is - God, in whatever way we experience or understand Him, as our creator - and the task seems to be to help people recognise Him at work in their own situation, in their own life, and to respond in the best way they know how. Nor does it follow that they have to identify with a Church to do it.

The spirit of God calls us to a new vision of Himself and His people and to the need to recognise that, to use a well-known Scottish phrase, 'we are all Jock Tamson's bairns', and that in some measure we are all in the Church, because we are all in His world. God is the creator of all and Jesus died for all, not just a select few. When we recognise this - when we see each other not as potential sons and daughters, but already within the family framework, however immature - it is then we will be taking the first step toward recognising a religious framework into which everybody fits and which is already hinted at a long time before Jesus ever set foot on this planet, when in the book of the prophet Isaiah we hear: 'My temple will be called a house of prayer for all nations. The Lord said to me, "I have a greater task for you, my servant - I will make you a light to the nations." '

This philosophy of life is indelibly stamped with the authority not of the Church but of Christ, who said, 'I have come that you may have life and have it more abundantly.'

To say that the spirit of God is blowing only in the minds of those who know God through Christ is surely to limit the power of that same spirit to move where it will and in diverse ways. If that is not in fact the case, then how do we account for all the effort and debate expended in the search for peace and understanding in this world? How do we account for the Bob Geldofs of our time or the relentless striving to save those in the Third World, as it has been dubbed, through the many agencies, religious and otherwise, in this and other countries? Or is it that we credit such action to be whims and fancies of man? Try telling those who work in extremely difficult and poorly paid conditions (some with no pay at all) that it is simply because they care, they are bothered and want desperately to do something about each and every situation before it becomes a tragedy, as often happens.

Let us pray, as indeed others in varying cultures do, that as well as belonging to those frameworks into which we have all been born and bred, we are equally part of that larger framework wherein God is ruler and Lord of all. Yes, even of those who claim to have no framework at all, and who do not openly acknowledge Him in the way we feel is appropriate.

This can only come about when we broaden our vision and extend our horizons. It can be most disturbing for some, when subjects like 'open communion' and 'baptism for all children' are effectively ignored. They are terms which tend to rock the boat and the boat cannot and must not be diverted from her 'established' true course. Remarriage is frowned upon as though those concerned had an acute attack of some contagious disease. When we ask questions about the Church and what it is all about, the common folk are not even consulted, and when they are little notice is taken of their point of view – nobody does anything about their dilemmas.

What many do not try to understand is that some parts of what might be regarded as most unorthodox doctrine are views firmly held within the context of Christ's ministry, and are invariably practised because that is, in their faithful and honest opinion, what God is calling them to do. It is not done without careful thought and prayer, and when it is done it brings nothing but a workload with which one finds it most difficult to cope, a load which very few are prepared to share. But Jesus said that his burden was light and so it is because it all becomes something of a privilege to be able to share something of God's love with those who have nothing.

It is this writer's belief that the spirit of God is calling us to reassess our understanding of His ways and the people who belong to Him. To embrace a family under God, in which every nation and every individual has their rightful place, is an ideal enshrined in the two commandments of Jesus: to love God and our neighbour. There is a need to assure people that they are important enough to take, for free, the place that is rightly theirs, and which the Church from time to time tries to withhold from its rightful owners. If we fail to grasp this vision, and, indeed, put it into practice, then any work we seek to do on behalf of our underprivileged brothers and sisters - all the effort used in seeking to aid the poor and needy, all the exercises in caring for the handicapped, the sick, and the blind, any missionary zeal extended throughout the world during the festive seasons of the year to show that God cares, indeed, anything at all done to assist in the nourishment not only of the underdogs, but of the common folk - all will be seen as a sham. Especially if our action does not assure each and every soul that it is done not because we want to win them for Christ, but so that His dying and rising reminds them of their rightful place within God's family.

Let all these things be done primarily because our faith says that God is their Father as well as ours.